DATE DUE

JUN 2 4 2006			
JUL 1 7 2009			
OCT 2 2012			
APR 0 4 2017			
OD 3-28-18			

Demco, Inc. 38-293

On the Front Line

SPYING AND THE COLD WAR

Michael Burgan

Chicago, Illinois

Produced for Raintree Publishers by Discovery Books Ltd
Editorial: Kathryn Walker, Juliet Smith, and Daniel Nunn
Design: Rob Norridge and Michelle Lisseter
Picture Research: Elaine Fuoco-Lang and Amy Sparks
Project Manager: Juliet Smith
Production: Duncan Gilbert
Printed and bound in China by South China Printing Company Ltd
Originated by Dot Gradations Ltd

10 09 08 07 06
10 9 8 7 6 5 4 3 2 1

Library of Congress Cataloging-in-Publication Data
Burgan, Michael
   Spying and the Cold War / Michael Burgan.
      p. cm. -- (Freestyle express) (On the front line)
   Includes bibliographical references and index.
   ISBN 1-4109-2195-6 (library bdg. hardcover) --
   ISBN 1-4109-2202-2 (pbk.)1. Espionage--History--20th century--Juvenile literature. 2. Cold War--Juvenile literature. I. Title. II. Series. III. Series: On the front line
UB270.5.B875 2006
327.1209'045--dc22
                                                 2005029587

This leveled text is a version of *Freestyle: On the Front Line: Spying and the Cold War*

Original edition produced by White-Thomson Publishing Ltd, Bridgewater Business Centre, 210 High Street, Lewes BN7 2NH, United Kingdom.

Acknowledgments
The publishers would like to thank the following for permission to reproduce photographs:
AKG pp. 9, 14(l), 16, 29; Corbis pp. 5, 10, 11, 19, 20, 23, 24, 26, 28, 31, 32–33, 34, 35, 37, 38, 39, 41; Novosti p. 40; Popperfoto p. 22; Topfoto pp. 4, 6, 8, 12, 14–15, 17, 18, 25, 27, 30, 36; United States National Archives and Records p. 21.
Cover photograph of espionage collage reproduced with permission of Corbis.

Maps on pp. 7, 13 by Peter Bull.

Source notes: pp. 4–5 *Contact on Gorky Street*, p. 13; p. 18 the All POW-MIA website, at www.aiipowmia.com/koreacw/powers.html, accessed 2/8/04; pp. 20–21 the CNN Cold War website at http://www.cnn.com/SPECIALS/cold.war/episodes/08/1st.draft/pravda.html, accessed 5/8/04; pp. 22–23 *Master of Disguise* by Antonio Mendez, p. 216; pp. 26–27 *Penkovsky Papers* by Penkovsky and *The Spy Who Saved the World* by Jerrold Schecter and Peter S. Deriabin; pp. 34–35 and pp. 38–39 CNN Cold War website, http://www.cnn.com/SPECIALS/cold.war/episodes/21/interviews/kalugin/ and http://www.cnn.com/SPECIALS/cold.war/episodes/22/script.html, accessed 7/8/04; pp. 40–41 *Secret Contenders* by Melvin Beck, p. 151.

Every effort has been made to contact copyright holders of any material reproduced in this book. Any omissions will be rectified in subsequent printings if notice is given to the publishers.

The paper used to print this book comes from sustainable resources.

CONTENTS

Any words appearing in the text in bold, **like this,** are explained in the glossary. You can also look out for them in the Word Bank box at the bottom of each page.

A BUSINESSMAN'S SECRET

What is Communism?

Communism is a system of government with only one political party. All land, businesses, and industries are owned by the state. Under **Communist** rule, equality is believed to be more important than personal freedom.

World War II ended in 1945. At this time, the **Soviet Union** was a huge country ruled by **Communism** (see panel on the left). The United States, Great Britain, and other countries were against Communism. They tried to stop this form of government from spreading. This struggle was called the "Cold War."

Cold War spies

Greville Wynne was a British businessman with a secret. He was also a spy for the British government. In 1960, Wynne visited the Soviet Union. He met with a Soviet army colonel named Oleg Penkovsky. Penkovsky wanted to spy for the **West**.

Oleg Penkovsky used special spy cameras. These cameras and their film were small enough to fit inside a cigarette pack (like the one pictured here). ➡

Word Bank   Communism one-party system of government where all property, businesses, and industries are owned by the state

Wynne and Penkovsky worked together. They told the British and U.S. governments secrets about the Soviet **military**, the country's fighting forces.

A dangerous game

The Soviets arrested Wynne and Penkovsky in 1962. Wynne was sentenced to eight years in prison for spying. But after two years, he was traded for a Soviet spy held in the United States. Penkovsky was executed for spying against his country.

After serving two years in prison in the Soviet Union for spying, Greville Wynne (center, in overcoat) was released in 1964.

Find out later

Who first used the phrase "Iron Curtain?"

Why were these supplies flown into a German city in 1948?

Which two world leaders helped end the Cold War?

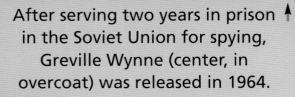

military a country's fighting forces, including the army, navy, and air force

THE COLD WAR BEGINS

Intelligence agencies

A country's **intelligence** agencies use spies to gather information on other countries. These agencies also try to protect their own country against spies. The major intelligence agencies of the Cold War included:

- Great Britain's **MI5** and **MI6**.
- The Soviet Union's **KGB** and **GRU**.
- The United States' **CIA** and **FBI**.
- East Germany's *Stasi.* East Germany was under Soviet control.

The **Soviet Union** was a group of states that included Russia. It was ruled by a **Communist** government based in Russia. Soviet leaders hoped to spread **Communism** around the world. But most Western nations did not want it.

World War II lasted from 1939 to 1945. During the war, the Soviet Union fought on the same side as Britain and the United States. At the end of the war, the Soviet army controlled most of Eastern Europe (see map on page 7).

British Prime Minister Winston Churchill (front left) meets with U.S. President Franklin D. Roosevelt (front center) and Soviet leader Joseph Stalin (front right). Their countries fought on the same side in World War II.

Word Bank Communist someone who supports Communism, a one-party system of government

The Iron Curtain

Western nations thought the Soviets were too powerful. In 1946, British Prime Minister Winston Churchill talked about an "Iron Curtain" in Europe (see map below). The Iron Curtain was the name given to the barrier between the **West** and Communist Eastern Europe.

The Cold War had begun. There was hostility between the East and the West. But the two sides did not fight. This is why it was called a "cold" war. Spying would play a big part in the struggle.

The Soviet Union

The Soviet Union existed from 1917 until 1991. It contained fifteen states. At the end of the Cold War in 1991, the Soviet states became fifteen **independent** nations. Russia was one of them.

This map shows European countries in 1946 and the Iron Curtain. It also shows the Iron Curtain in 1955. The "curtain" shows how Europe was divided between the Soviet-dominated East (colored gray) and the West (colored yellow).

West countries of Western Europe, North America, Australia, and New Zealand

The Manhattan Project

During World War II, scientists from Europe and the United States developed the **atomic bomb** (also called the **nuclear bomb**). This type of bomb is a weapon that causes enormous destruction.

The work took place in the United States. It was called the "Manhattan Project." In 1945, the United States dropped atomic bombs on two Japanese cities.

The spy

One scientist working on the Manhattan Project was a **Communist** spy. His name was Klaus Fuchs.

Nuclear weapons and the Cold War

During the Cold War, several nations built nuclear weapons. But the Americans and Soviets controlled most of these. Some people feared that the two enemies would start a war. A nuclear war would kill millions of people.

In August 1945, the United States dropped an atomic bomb on the Japanese city of Hiroshima. These soldiers are standing in the rubble of the destroyed city. ➡

Word Bank nuclear bomb extremely destructive bomb powered by the release of nuclear energy

8

Fuchs gave the Soviets some information they needed to build their own atomic bomb. In 1949, the Soviets tested their first atomic bomb.

Jailed

Fuchs moved to Britain in 1946. The **FBI** discovered that Fuchs was a spy. In 1950, he was sent to prison in Britain. After nine years, Fuchs was freed. He went to live in East Germany.

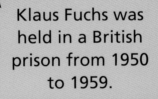

Klaus Fuchs was held in a British prison from 1950 to 1959.

FBI (Federal Bureau of Investigation) leading U.S. intelligence agency

Spies across the United States?

Joseph McCarthy was a U.S. **senator** in the 1950s. McCarthy believed that **Communists** were working in the U.S. government. He also believed Communists were working in U.S. companies. McCarthy said these people might be spies for the **Soviet Union**. Many Americans believed him.

McCarthy named several people whom he thought were Communists. But he never produced evidence that any of them were spies.

Some Americans who hated **Communism** thought Joseph McCarthy was a hero. He is pictured here, pointing to a map.

COMMUNIST PARTY ORGANIZATION U.S.A-FEB. 9, 1950

Word Bank   senator   one of 100 people elected to serve in the U.S. Senate

Hunting for Communists

In 1953, McCarthy led a committee to hunt for Communists. McCarthy also claimed that there were soldiers in the U.S. army who were acting as spies. He felt they were spying for the Soviet Union.

Again, McCarthy could not support his claims. Some Americans began to doubt what he said. By the end of 1954, McCarthy had lost his power. But by that time, his claims had ruined the careers of many well-known Americans.

During the late 1940s and early 1950s, some people believed these famous American movie stars were Communists. They are, from left to right, Paul Henreid, Lauren Bacall, Danny Kaye, and Humphrey Bogart. ↓

English spies

Guy Burgess and Donald Maclean studied at Cambridge University in England. After they left Cambridge, both worked for the British government as spies. Burgess and Maclean were also spying for the Soviet Union. In 1951 they went to live in the Soviet Union. They wanted to avoid arrest in England for **treason**.

treason crime of doing something to harm one's own government

FIRST CONFLICTS

Berlin divided

After World War II, Germany was divided into four areas. The British, Americans, French, and Soviets each controlled one area of Germany.

The German capital of Berlin was in the Soviet area. But Berlin was also divided up. The **Soviet Union** controlled East Berlin. East Berlin was **Communist**. The other powers controlled West Berlin. West Berlin was not Communist.

In June 1948, Soviet spies discovered that the Western nations planned to join their areas together.

The Korean War

The Asian country of Korea (see map on page 13) was divided after World War II. Soviets controlled North Korea. The United States controlled the South. In 1950, North Korean troops invaded the South. The Korean War had started. The United States and other countries sent troops to help the South. The Korean War ended in 1953 when the Communists failed to defeat South Korea.

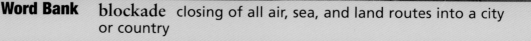

The Berlin Airlift continued all through the winter of 1948–1949. Here, workers are unloading the one millionth sack of coal to arrive in Berlin.

Word Bank blockade closing of all air, sea, and land routes into a city or country

They also planned to join their areas in Berlin. Joseph Stalin, the Soviet leader, was against this.

The Berlin airlift

Stalin began a **blockade**. He closed all the roads, railroads, and canals into West Berlin. Supplies could not reach West Berlin by land or by water.

To defeat the blockade, American and British planes flew supplies into West Berlin. This **airlift** kept West Berliners alive until Stalin ended the blockade in May 1949.

This map shows where there was conflict during the Cold War.

Airlift facts

During the Soviet blockade, tons of supplies had to be flown into Berlin. West Berlin had a population of 2.3 million. To get enough supplies to the people, planes arrived every 90 seconds. The highest number of flights in one day was 1,398.

Conflict during the Cold War

airlift use of many planes to bring people or goods in and out of a place

George Blake

George Blake was a spy for British **MI6**. In 1953, he became a **double agent**. He began to spy for the **Soviet Union**.

A secret tunnel

In 1953, Blake heard about plans to build a tunnel under East Berlin. East Berlin was under Soviet control. British and U.S. **intelligence** would use the tunnel. They could listen in to telephone lines and hear Soviet secrets.

↑ East German soldiers inside the Berlin spy tunnel.

Word Bank double agent agent for one country who also spies for another country

Blake told the Soviets about the tunnel. But the Soviets did not stop it from being built. They did not want anyone to guess Blake was spying for them.

The Soviets allowed the **Allies** to hear a mix of real and false information. The Soviets closed the tunnel in 1956. They pretended they had just found it.

Spy uncovered

In 1961, the British discovered Blake was helping the Soviets. He was sent to prison in England. Blake escaped and went to live in the Soviet Union.

The Berlin Wall

Many East Germans wanted to escape **Communism**. To do this, they went to East Berlin and then crossed into West Berlin. West Berlin was controlled by Western powers.

In 1961, the East Germans started building a wall between East and West Berlin. East Germans trying to cross the wall were shot.

◄ This photo shows the Berlin Wall in 1962. The wall reminded people that **Communist** governments limited freedom. It was knocked down in 1989.

Allies Western countries, including Great Britain and the United States, that were friends and worked closely together

Alliances

A group of Western nations joined together to stop **Communism** from spreading through Europe. These countries included the United States and Britain. They formed the **North Atlantic Treaty Organization (NATO)** in 1949.

In response, the **Soviet Union** formed the **Warsaw Pact** in 1955. This was a group of **Communist** nations that were controlled by the Soviet Union.

Trouble in Hungary

Hungary (see map on page 13) was a member of the Warsaw Pact. In October 1956, Hungarians

Armed Hungarians stand in front of a **military** vehicle during the 1956 **rebellion**.

Word Bank protest show disagreement through organized action, such as a march or demonstration

protested against their government. They wanted an end to Soviet rule. They wanted more freedom. Soviet troops marched into Hungary to stop the protests.

The KGB takes charge

Imre Nagy became leader of Hungary in October 1956. But he also wanted to weaken Soviet rule in Hungary. In November, Nagy was arrested by members of the Soviet **KGB**.

Nagy was replaced by Janos Kadar. Kadar followed Soviet orders. In 1958, the KGB executed Nagy.

The CIA in action

Like the Soviet KGB, the American **CIA** was involved in changing foreign governments. In the 1950s, the CIA helped remove leaders in Iran and Guatemala (see map on page 13). The CIA felt that these leaders were too friendly with the Soviet Union.

In 1956, these Hungarian protesters drove through the streets of Budapest on top of a tank. But the Soviets soon crushed their rebellion.

KGB (Committee for State Security) leading intelligence agency in the Soviet Union

TOOLS OF THE TRADE

On May 1, 1960, Francis Gary Powers soared 68,000 feet (20,730 meters) above the **Soviet Union**. He was flying a U-2 spy plane. Powers had a special camera for photographing Soviet **military** sites. He was a U.S. spy working for the **CIA**.

Shot down and caught

Suddenly, a Soviet missile exploded near the plane. The plane began to fall. The Americans did not know the Soviets had missiles that could reach this height.

Powers parachuted out of his burning plane. He was arrested by the Soviet **KGB**.

Spy in the sky

Here are some facts about the American U-2 spy plane:

Length:
63 feet (19.2 meters)

Height:
16 feet (4.8 meters)

Wingspan:
105 feet (32 meters)

Speed:
more than 475 mph (764 km/h)

Altitude:
above 70,000 feet (21,212) meters

Crew: 1

U.S. pilots flew the U-2 spy plane throughout the Cold War. They used the planes to take secret photographs high above other countries.

Word Bank   military a country's fighting forces, including the army, navy, and air force

U.S. pilot Francis Gary Powers (standing), after his capture. He is facing a Soviet court for spying from a U-2 plane.

Spy trade

The Soviets were angry that the Americans had sent spy planes over the Soviet Union. They sent Powers to prison. In 1962 the Soviets agreed to a trade. They released Powers in return for a Soviet spy held in the United States.

altitude distance above sea level

This chart compares the *Sputnik* and *Corona* satellites:

Sputnik
(Soviet Union)

Launched:
October 4, 1957
Altitude: 500 miles
(800 kilometers)
Speed: 18,000 mph
(28,800 km/h)

Corona
(United States)

Launched:
August 18, 1960
Altitude: more than
100 miles
(160 kilometers)
Speed: more than
17,000 mph
(27,000 km/h)

This photo shows the U.S. *Atlas* rocket on its launchpad. The rocket was used to launch ICBMs. →

Sputnik enters space

During the 1950s, both the United States and the **Soviet Union** built many large missiles. In May 1957, the Soviets tested their first large missile. It was an **intercontinental ballistic missile (ICBM)**. This meant it could travel great distances.

In October 1957, the Soviets fired one of these new missiles into space. It carried a **satellite** called *Sputnik* that circled Earth.

Word Bank intercontinental ballistic missile (ICBM) missile that can travel great distances and carry one or more nuclear weapons

U.S. leaders were shocked. The Soviets now had a missile powerful enough to attack the United States. It could be used to carry nuclear **warheads**.

Spying in space

The United States soon built its own ICBMs and launched satellites. In 1960, the United States launched a satellite called *Corona*. Satellites circle Earth and send back information. This satellite took pictures of **Communist** countries.

Satellites played an important part in Cold War spying. They helped both sides learn more about each other.

The U.S. satellite *Corona* took this picture of the Kremlin in the Soviet Union. The Kremlin was the home of the Soviet government.

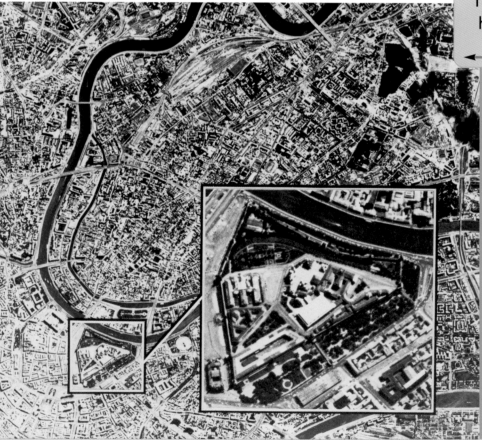

warhead the part of a missile that explodes

Avoiding the KGB

Antonio Mendez was an **agent** for a U.S. **intelligence** organization, the **CIA**. Mendez created disguises. In 1976, he went to Moscow. This was the Soviet capital. Mendez went to help the CIA work with a Soviet **double agent** called Trinity.

CIA agents in Moscow were usually followed by the Soviet **KGB**. U.S. agents looked for ways to avoid the KGB. Mendez helped them do this with disguises.

Spies sometimes used tiny guns to defend themselves. This gun is so small it will fit into a cigarette pack.

Word Bank   double agent agent for one country who also spies for another country

Clever disguise

A U.S. agent needed to meet Trinity. Mendez created a disguise for the agent. He gave him a wig, a fake moustache, and Soviet clothes. He used a clay-like material to change the shape of the agent's nose. The agent safely met Trinity. The disguise worked.

The death of Trinity

In 1977, the KGB found out that Trinity was a double agent. They arrested him, but Trinity killed himself. He bit into a pen filled with poison.

The Kremlin was the home of the Soviet government. In 1989, CIA agents put a listening device in a tunnel underneath the Kremlin. The device allowed the CIA to listen to conversations between Soviet politicians.

CIA (Central Intelligence Agency) leading U.S. intelligence agency

CRISIS IN CUBA

Cuba is just 90 miles (145 kilometers) away from the U.S. coast (see map on page 13). In 1959, Fidel Castro became the leader of Cuba.

Castro ended U.S. control of Cuba. The United States refused to trade with Cuba. Castro traded with the **Soviet Union** instead.

Finding Soviet missiles

In October 1962, a U-2 spy plane took pictures of Cuba. These showed Soviet nuclear missiles on the island. U.S. President John F. Kennedy told the

The CIA in Cuba

The **CIA** tried to kill Fidel Castro many times. The CIA also trained a group of Cubans to fight Castro. These Cubans lived in the United States. In 1961, the group invaded Cuba at a place called the Bay of Pigs. They were defeated by Castro's army.

Fidel Castro (center, with beard) and a group of **rebels** took power in Cuba. They replaced leaders who had been friendly with the United States.

Word Bank rebel person who fights against those who are in power

Soviets to remove the missiles. The Soviet leader, Nikita Krushchev, refused.

Preventing a war

Troops prepared to fight while the two leaders talked. Finally, the Soviet Union agreed to remove its missiles from Cuba. The United States promised not to invade Cuba.

For a while, people everywhere had been scared. They knew that if the two sides had gone to war, there could have been a terrible nuclear war.

MISSILE TRANSPORTERS

HEAVY EQUIPMENT

12 MISSILES

5 MISSILE TRANSPORTERS

MISSILE TRANSPORTERS

This photo from a U-2 spy plane, taken in October 1962, shows the Soviet missiles in Cuba.

OPEN STORAGE

A daring request

On August 12, 1960, a Soviet man approached two American tourists in Moscow. The man gave the Americans a letter. He asked the Americans to give the letter to U.S. officials in Moscow.

The Soviet man was Oleg Penkovsky. He was a colonel in the **GRU**. The GRU was a Soviet **intelligence** agency. Penkovsky wanted to become a **double agent**. He wanted to spy for the **West**.

The Soviet Union wanted the West to think that missiles such as these were **accurate**. Oleg Penkovsky told the officials in the West that this was not always true.

Word Bank   accurate   able to hit a target

Penkovsky soon met with **agents** from the American **CIA** and British **MI6**. He told them secrets about Soviet nuclear weapons.

End of a spy

In 1962, Soviet officials began to suspect Penkovsky. They thought he was a double agent. Soviet agents hid cameras in his apartment. They watched him closely.

Eventually, the **KGB** arrested Penkovsky. In May 1963, Penkovsky was shot and killed.

Oleg Penkovsky (left) was found guilty of spying against his own country. In May 1963, he was shot and killed.

During the Cold War, the **Soviet Union** and the United States used other countries to help them. These countries were called **proxies**. Proxy nations produced several "super spies." These were spies who collected useful information over many years.

Günter Guillaume

Günter Guillaume was a super spy. East Germany was under Soviet control. The East German **intelligence** agency was called the *Stasi*. In 1956, the *Stasi* sent Guillaume to West Germany.

Word Bank   proxy   person or country working for another person or country

Guillaume helped the West German leader. But he also gave the Soviets information about West German politics. Guillaume was caught in 1974. He was later traded for two West German spies held in East Germany.

The Polish super spy

Ryszard Kuklinski was another super spy. He was a colonel in the Polish army. Kuklinski worked closely with the Soviet Union. For almost ten years, he also spied for the **West**. He moved to the United States in 1981.

Satellite dishes such as this helped countries pick up messages from both their allies and their enemies.

Günter Guillaume (right) worked closely with West German leader Willy Brandt (left). But Guillaume was also a super spy working for East Germany.

intelligence government services that spy on other countries. The word also refers to the information spies gather.

Double agent

The **Soviet Union** sent Dmitri Polyakov to New York City in 1951. Polyakov worked at the **United Nations (UN)**. He was told to spy on the United States. But Polyakov began to dislike the Soviet government.

In 1961, Polyakov became a top **double agent** for the United States. He gave the **FBI** the names of many Soviet **intelligence agents** around the world.

The United Nations

The United Nations (UN) was created in 1945. Countries sent representatives to the United Nations to talk about world problems. The countries hoped this would help prevent wars. But some countries sent intelligence agents to work at the UN. Then they could spy for their countries.

The United Nations meets at this building in New York City. During the Cold War, Soviet and U.S. officials often argued here. →

30

Word Bank double agent agent for one country who also spies for another country

Useful information

During the Cold War, both the United States and Soviet Union made dangerous weapons. Polyakov told the Americans about Soviet weapons. He gave the Soviets false information about U.S. weapons.

The game is up

In 1985, the Russians found out that Polyakov was spying for the Americans. At that time, Polyakov was back in the Soviet Union. He was executed for **treason**.

U.S. and Soviet soldiers were trained to deal with dangerous weapons. Some weapons used chemicals, germs, or diseases to kill people. Spies from both sides tried to find out about these new weapons.

treason   crime of doing something to harm one's own government

DIFFICULT DECADES

In 1954, the Asian country of Vietnam (see map on page 13) was split in two. **Communists** controlled North Vietnam. They were supported by the **Soviet Union** and China. The leaders of South Vietnam were against **Communism**. They were supported by the United States.

The Vietnam War

In 1959, Communists in South Vietnam began fighting their government. These fighters were called the **Viet Cong**. North Vietnam sent weapons and supplies to the Viet Cong.

South Vietnamese troops attack a Viet Cong village in South Vietnam.

Word Bank   Viet Cong Communist rebels in South Vietnam

The United States sent help to South Vietnam. From 1965 to 1973, U.S. soldiers fought in Vietnam. The fighting spread to the neighboring countries of Laos and Cambodia.

Spying in Vietnam

U.S. **intelligence** agencies worked with the South Vietnamese. They tried to find Viet Cong leaders. In Laos, the **CIA** organized an army. These soldiers fought North Vietnamese troops that entered Laos.

U.S. troops in Vietnam

The number of U.S. troops in Vietnam grew quickly after 1963.

1959	760
1963	16,000
1966	385,300
1968	536,000
1971	156,800
1973	50
1975	Last troops leave Saigon, the capital of South Vietnam

Communism one-party system of government where all property, businesses, and industries are owned by the state

Helping the enemy

Intelligence played a very important part in the Vietnam War. A U.S. sailor named John Walker was a spy for the **Communists**. He worked at an important naval office.

In 1967, Walker offered to give the Soviets secret **codes**. Codes are patterns of letters or numbers used to send secret messages. Walker wanted money for this information.

These codes helped the Soviets in Vietnam. U.S. planes often bombed targets in North

Walker and his spy ring supplied codes to the Soviet Union. These codes allowed the Soviets to track U.S. ships and submarines.

Word Bank KGB (Committee for State Security) leading intelligence agency in the Soviet Union

Vietnam. The codes allowed the Communists to find out which targets the United States were planning to bomb.

A million secrets

Walker persuaded three others to become spies. They worked together. They formed a spy ring. American leaders did not find out about this spy ring until 1985. By then, the ring had helped the Soviets read more than one million U.S. messages.

The **KGB** said that Walker had been its most important spy during the Cold War.

Money for secrets

The **Soviet Union** used several spies in the U.S. armed forces. Many spies in the **West** believed in **Communism**. But some spies just wanted to make money. John Walker earned up to $4,000 a month as a spy.

John Walker (front left) was sent to prison for life in 1985 for helping the Soviets. The other three members of his spy ring were also sent to prison.

Trouble in Afghanistan

In 1978, a **Communist** government came to power in Afghanistan. Afghanistan bordered the **Soviet Union** in the south (see map on page 13). The Soviet Union supported this government.

But there was conflict. Communists were against religion. Most Afghans were **Muslims**. Muslims follow the religion called **Islam**. Many Afghan Muslims fought their Communist government.

Soviet invasion

In 1979, it looked as if Afghanistan's leader, Hafizullah Amin, was losing the war. Soviet troops

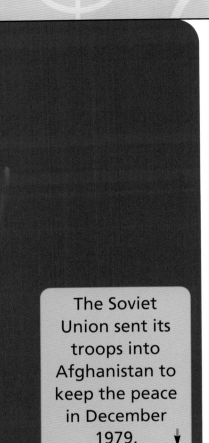

The Soviet Union sent its troops into Afghanistan to keep the peace in December 1979.

Word Bank   Muslims followers of Islam

moved into Afghanistan. **KGB** agents killed Amin. Soviet troops stayed in the country to keep the peace.

The Soviet invasion of Afghanistan angered the United States. From 1980 to 1989, U.S. Presidents Jimmy Carter and Ronald Reagan sent weapons and supplies to the Muslim fighters.

Soviet troops leave

In 1989, the Soviet Union removed its troops. The war had cost the Soviets too much money and too many soldiers.

Between 1979 and 1989, Afghan Muslims of all ages fought against the Soviets.

The Taliban

In the 1990s, Afghan Muslims called the Taliban took power in Afghanistan. The Taliban supported a **terrorist** named Osama bin Laden. On September 11, 2001, bin Laden's terrorists destroyed the World Trade Center in New York City. Almost 3,000 Americans died.

terrorist   person who uses violence for political or religious reasons

REACHING THE END

In 1982, U.S. President Ronald Reagan spoke of the **Soviet Union** as an "evil empire." He often talked about ending **Communism**. The Soviet **KGB** believed that Reagan was planning a nuclear war against the Soviet Union.

Oleg Gordievsky

Oleg Gordievsky worked for the KGB in London. But he also worked for Britain's **MI6**. Gordievsky and other Soviet **agents** were told to watch for signs that the **West** was preparing for war.

This U.S. nuclear missile is called a *Lance* missile. During the Cold War, the West had missiles like this ready to use if war broke out in Eastern Europe. ➡

Word Bank   North Atlantic Treaty Organization (NATO)   group of Western nations led by the United States

Ending the fears

In November 1983 **NATO** troops held war games in parts of Europe. War games are a form of training that prepares soldiers for real war. Soviet leaders saw the "games" as proof that the West planned to attack them.

Gordievsky was worried. He thought Soviet leaders might start a nuclear war to prevent an attack. He told Western officials what the Soviets believed.

The Americans saw how their tough talk had worried the Soviets. President Reagan decided to try to improve relations with the Soviet Union.

Toward the end of the Cold War, the United States and the Soviet Union destroyed their **intercontinental ballistic missiles (ICBMs)**. These U.S. soldiers are using explosives to destroy two **warheads**. The year is 1987.

intercontinental ballistic missile (ICBM) missile that can travel great distances and carry one or more nuclear weapons

39

Getting rid of weapons

During the 1980s, the United States produced many new weapons. The **Soviet Union** could not afford to build as many weapons. Soviet leader Mikhail Gorbachev met with U.S. President Ronald Reagan. Both leaders agreed to get rid of some of their nuclear weapons.

The Wall comes down

Many countries in Eastern Europe were under Soviet control. Gorbachev gave these countries more **independence**. By 1989, most of them had

Time line – the end of the Cold War

1985 – Mikhail Gorbachev takes power in the Soviet Union.

1987 – The Soviet Union and the United States agree to remove many nuclear weapons from Europe.

1989 – Communist governments fall in several Eastern European countries. The Berlin Wall comes down.

1990 – East and West Germany unite. The Soviet Union begins to break apart. It splits into fifteen separate nations.

Ronald Reagan (center) and Mikhail Gorbachev (left) met several times. They are seen here in Moscow in 1988.

Word Bank   independence   freedom to act as one chooses

decided they did not want **Communism**. The Berlin Wall (see page 15) was knocked down in 1989. In 1990, East and West Germany joined together and became one nation. **Communist** rule in Germany had ended.

End of the Soviet Union

People in the Soviet Union also wanted more freedom. In 1990, some Soviet states began to demand independence. By late 1991, the Soviet Union ceased to exist. The Cold War was over.

Spies today

The Cold War is over. But the **West** and Russia still use spies. Many spies help in the fight against **terrorists**.

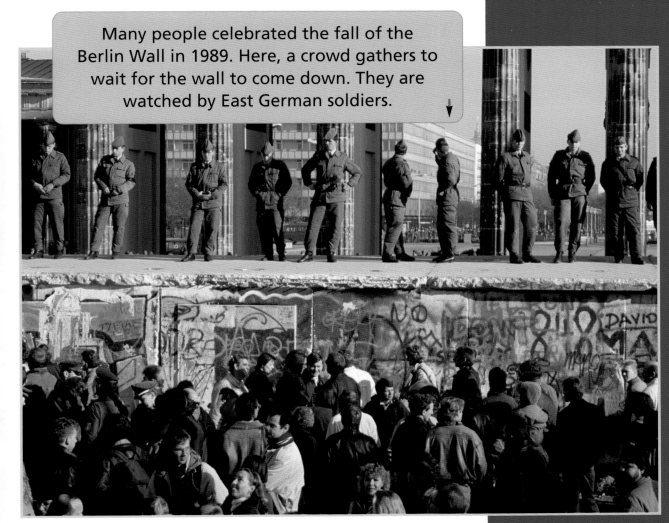

Many people celebrated the fall of the Berlin Wall in 1989. Here, a crowd gathers to wait for the wall to come down. They are watched by East German soldiers.

TIME LINE

1917   **Communists** take control of the Russian government.

1939   World War II begins.

1945   The United States drops the world's first two **nuclear bombs** on Hiroshima and Nagasaki in Japan.
World War II ends and the Cold War begins.
The **United Nations** is formed.

1948   U.S. and British planes bring supplies to West Berlin.

1949   The United States and eleven other Western nations form **NATO**.
Communists take power in China.

1950   U.S. senator Joseph McCarthy accuses many U.S. government workers of spying for the Soviets.
North Korea uses Soviet help to invade South Korea.

1951   British **double agents** Guy Burgess and Donald Maclean go to live in Moscow.

1953   Julius and Ethel Rosenberg are executed for spying against the United States.
The **CIA** helps replace the government in Iran.
The Korean War ends.

1954   The CIA defeats a government in Guatemala that works with Communists.
Vietnam is divided into two nations.

1955   The **West** opens a spy tunnel under East Berlin.
The **Soviet Union** and seven other Communist nations form the **Warsaw Pact**.

1956	Soviet forces and **KGB agents** help end protests against Communist rule in Hungary.
1957	The Soviet Union launches the first **satellite**.
1959	Fidel Castro takes power in Cuba.
1960	U.S. pilot Francis Gary Powers is shot down in a U-2 spy plane over the Soviet Union. The United States launches the world's first spy satellite.
1961	The CIA helps **rebels** invade Cuba. The rebels are defeated. The Soviets and East Germans build the Berlin Wall.
1962	The Soviet Union places nuclear missiles in Cuba. A U-2 spy plane notices the missiles. The Soviets agree to remove them. Soviet double agent Oleg Penkovsky is arrested for spying for the West.
1965	U.S. troops arrive in South Vietnam.
1975	The Vietnam War ends.
1979	Soviet troops invade Afghanistan.
1985	Mikhail Gorbachev comes to power in the Soviet Union.
1987	The United States and the Soviet Union agree to remove many nuclear weapons from Europe.
1989	Communist governments fall in several Eastern European countries. The Berlin Wall is torn down.
1991	The Cold War ends.

FIND OUT MORE

Organizations

International Spy Museum
This museum focuses on the important role that spying has played in world events. Exhibits include a large collection of gadgets used for spying. Historical photos, audiovisual programs, and interactive displays tell the stories of some of the most secret spying missions in history. You can contact the museum at the following address:
800 F Street, NW Washington, DC 20004

Books

Sherman, Josepha. *The Cold War (Chronicles of America's Wars)*. Minneapolis Minn.: Lerner Publications, 2003.

Collier, Christopher and James Lincoln. *The United States and the Cold War 1945–1989 (Drama of American History)*. New York: Benchmark Books, 2001.

Stanley, George E. *America and the Cold War: 1949–1969 (A Primary Source History of the United States)*. Milwaukee: World Almanac, 2005.

DVD/VHS

Films about spying are often aimed at an adult audience. Ask a parent or teacher before watching these.

Declassified: The Inside Story of American Espionage Agencies (VHS, 2000)
A four-part documentary that looks at the fascinating activities of U.S. intelligence agencies.

Secrets, Lies and Atomic Spies (VHS, 2002)
A documentary about Soviet spies working in the United States.

World Wide Web

To find out more about the Cold War and spying you can search the Internet. Use keywords such as these:
- "Manhattan Project"
- Cold War + espionage
- "Berlin spy tunnel"

You can find your own keywords by using words from this book. The search tips below will help you find useful Web sites.

Search tips

There are billions of pages on the Internet. It can be difficult to find exactly what you are looking for. These tips will help you find useful Web sites more quickly:
- Know what you want to find out about.
- Use simple keywords.
- Use two to six keywords in a search.
- Only use names of people, places, or things.
- Put double quotation marks around words that go together, for example, "Berlin Airlift."

Where to search

Search engine
A search engine looks through millions of Web site pages. It lists all the sites that match the words in the search box. You will find the best matches are at the top of the list, on the first page.

Search directory
A person instead of a computer has sorted a search directory. You can search by keyword or subject and browse through the different sites. It is like looking through books on a library shelf.

45

GLOSSARY

accurate able to hit a target

agent spy or someone who works with spies and helps gather intelligence

airlift use of many planes to bring people or goods in and out of a place

Allies Western countries, including Great Britain and the United States, that were friends and worked closely together

altitude distance above sea level

atomic bomb *see* nuclear bomb

blockade closing of all air, sea, and land routes into a city or country

CIA (Central Intelligence Agency) leading U.S. intelligence agency

code pattern of letters or numbers used to send secret messages

Communism one-party system of government where all property, businesses, and industries are owned by the state

Communist someone who supports Communism, a one-party system of government

double agent agent for one country who also spies for another country

FBI (Federal Bureau of Investigation) leading U.S. intelligence agency

GRU (Main Intelligence Administration) East German intelligence agency

independence freedom to act as one chooses

independent having freedom to act as one chooses

intelligence government services that spy on other countries. The word also refers to the information that spies gather.

intercontinental ballistic missile (ICBM) missile that can travel great distances and carry one or more nuclear weapons

Islam religion based on the ideas of the Prophet Mohammed

KGB (Committee for State Security) leading intelligence agency in the Soviet Union

MI5 (Military Intelligence 5) British agency responsible for protecting Great Britain against internal threats to its security

MI6 (Military Intelligence 6) British agency responsible for protecting Great Britain against foreign threats to its security

military a country's fighting forces including the army, navy, and air force

Muslims followers of Islam

North Atlantic Treaty Organization (NATO) group of Western nations led by the United States

nuclear bomb extremely destructive bomb powered by the release of nuclear energy

protest show disagreement through organized action, such as a march or demonstration

proxy person or country working for another person or country

rebel person who fights against those who are in power

rebellion use of violence to force a change in government

satellite object that circles the Earth sending back various kinds of information

senator one of 100 people elected to serve in the U.S. Senate

Soviet Union country that once spread across northern Asia into Eastern Europe and included what is now Russia

Stasi **(Ministry of State Security)** East Germany's main secret police and intelligence agency

terrorist person who uses violence for political or religious reasons

treason crime of doing something to harm one's own government

United Nations (UN) organization made up of many countries. The UN tries to solve world problems in a peaceful way.

Viet Cong Communist rebels in South Vietnam

warhead the part of a missile that explodes

Warsaw Pact group of Communist nations controlled by the Soviet Union

West countries of Western Europe, North America, Australia, and New Zealand

INDEX